I0470582

Dig Your Work:
The Plan for Job
Satisfaction

David DeFord

Ordinary People Can Win!
Omaha, NE

1

Copyright

Copyright © 2013 by David DeFord
All rights reserved. No part of this book may be
reproduced in any form or by any electronic or
mechanical means including information storage and
retrieval systems – except in the case of brief
quotations in articles or reviews – without the
permission in writing from its publisher, your name.
All brand names and product names used in this book
are trademarks, registered trademarks, or trade names
of their respective holders. We are not associated with
any product or vendor in this book.

10 9 8 7 6 5 4 3 2 1

David and Kathy DeFord
13964 Margo Street
Omaha, NE 68138
david@daviddeford.com

Dedication

To Roger Wells who taught me to own my career.

The only way to do great work is to love what you do.

Steve Jobs

Introduction

Years ago I listened to my teenaged son and his friend talking together in the backseat of the car as I drove them to an event. I heard Willie's friend ask him, "What does your dad do for work?" I wanted to hear Willie's reply. I will never forget his answer, "I don't know, but whatever it is, I don't want to do it."

This simple, honest reply broke my heart. I felt not only discouraged because he was right, I didn't love my job. But I also felt ashamed that my griping about my work gave my four children horrible impressions about work—its something to endure until the weekend, the next vacation, or retirement. I didn't want my kids to view their work life that negatively.

I also realized my only actions I took regarding my job dissatisfaction was complaining. That actually compounded the impact. I wanted my kids to understand that work can be a meaningful part of one's life. But I wasn't setting that example.

I challenge you to do better than I did. Commit yourself to taking active steps to improve each negative area of your work life.

Take responsibility for your happiness at work.

Own your career, and your career happiness.

Dig your work.

Part I

What Are You Doing About It?

Take Personal Responsibility

Profit is a by-product of work; happiness is its chief product.

Henry Ford

As I travel all across the U.S. and Canada, I overhear conversations in airports, on airplanes, during seminar breaks, and in hotels. I love listening to people discuss their work. I notice that when a person discusses work with someone who does not work in the same organization, they speak more positively.

But when speaking to a coworker the gloves come off. They gripe about their bosses. They complain about their coworkers. They criticize their customers, the workload, and the lack of communication, respect, and autonomy. They even whine about negativity!

I decided to do a little research. As I speak to audiences I ask each audience member to identify three things they love about their work and three things they don't love about it. After we discuss what they don't love, I surprise them by asking, "What are you doing about these things?"

My mission is to help you love your work.

If you want to turn away from the dark side into the light, if you want to take responsibility for your love affair with your work, if you want to find delight in this important part of your life, then read this book. I know it can help you.

I help people dig their work by:
- Giving simple and researched tips on blog entries at least weekly
- Publishing an e-mail newsletter that features additional tips and recommended resources for further study
- Hosting webinar discussions so you can bring up questions and help each other
- Hosting daylong public seminars to give concentrated advice and Q&A
- Offering private seminars for organizations needing a lift
- Presenting keynote addresses to associations

If you want to join me in this worthwhile endeavor, just "Like" my Facebook page at http://www.facebook.com/digyourwork.

Pass it on! We can create a Dig Your Work movement!

Your Top Three Issues

People rarely succeed unless they have fun in what they are doing.

Dale Carnegie

List below three issues that keep you from enjoying your work. What three issues, if you could eliminate them or reduce their impact, would bring you the biggest jump in your job satisfaction?

1.

2.

3.

I have polled more than 1100 people for their top three, and found the largest issues to be (percentages represent the percentage of people who indicated the issue):

- Ineffective or unsupportive leaders (26%)
- Difficult coworkers (25%)
- Stress and time constraints (21%)

Since most people look for someone else to fix work issues for him or her, I decided to write this book to encourage you to take accountability for your happiness at work. Almost never will someone else take care of these things for you.

You own your career. Make it something you enjoy.

Own Your Career

*Happiness is the meaning and the purpose of life, the
whole aim and end of human existence.*
Aristotle

One of the sources of work frustration comes when
you wait for your employer to take care of you.
Trimmed budgets, increased workloads, and a
reduced workforce make it less likely that your boss
can approve everything you want.

Training, books, schedule accommodations, and other
requests may or may not be approved. But you own
your career. Why wait for others to provide what you
need?

Many people want someone else to take care of their
needs. When I lead two-day seminars, I notice a
consistent pattern. If an audience member complains
about the temperature, I ask the venue host to make
an adjustment. But often, the room stays too cold for
some of the participants. The next day, I try to notice
if the cold participant brings a sweater or other
additional layer. Rarely do they.

I recently had an audience member mention her
disgust that a 20-ounce diet soda cost her $2.50 at the

gift shop. I watched to see what she brought to drink on the second day. Nothing. She bought four of the sodas on the second day.

Many would rather complain rather than take personal action.

If you see the need for a change at work, look first at what you can do.

First Look at Yourself

Whoever is happy will make others happy.
Anne Frank

As you examine the things about your work that you don't like, be objective enough to first look at yourself. Are you contributing to, or creating the condition you don't like?

Say the negativity of your coworkers bothers you— are you part of the problem? Notice your own words for a week.

The top work frustration identified in my research is controlling and over-demanding bosses. If your boss micromanages you, have you assertively discussed it with him or her?

I once worked for Phil. His major characteristics were: micromanager, controlling personality, over-reacter, and perfectionist. Yikes! Finally, I made an appointment with Phil and told him, "I feel I have earned your trust, now I'm asking for it." I went on to explain the effect of his micromanaging and his overriding of my directions to my people. The session didn't go well—he blew up. However, after a few days I started to see a change in his approach toward me. He eased up. We talked about it several times after my first session with him. We worked out an acceptable working relationship.

Often your stress and discomfort can be overcome with personal action. Sometimes you need to learn something that will help: assertiveness, time management, conflict resolution, attitude lifting, etc.

Look at any situation that causes you to dislike your work. What can you do? What do you need to learn? Can this be improved? Can you live with it if you cannot change it.

First look at yourself as you review what you don't like at work. Take accountability. Take action.

Limits We Place on Ourselves

What we think determines what happens to us, so if we want to change our lives, we need to stretch our minds.

Dr. Wayne Dyer

Author, speaker, and trainer Zig Ziglar uses a powerful analogy to explain how we tend to settle for less than we want.

He tells how easily fleas may be trained. A lab technician places a number of fleas in a container, and covers it with a lid. Fleas jump, so when they first jump in the container, they collide with the lid. In a short time, the fleas make shorter jumps to avoid the pain of impact. In less than a day, the lab tech can remove the lid and the fleas continue making their short jumps. With no lid, they remain confined to the container. They have settled for less than they could do. They have the ability to escape from their confinement and afflict some poor animal or person, but they settle for less.

The fleas probably spend their social time complaining about their confinement. They don't seem to understand that they could escape if they chose.

We act like those fleas. We let our bosses put constraints on us, and we adjust our expectations. We don't like it and we complain, but we don't take action. We choose to settle for dissatisfaction, when we could take steps toward better job satisfaction.

Pinpoint your constraints, and choose to free yourself. Visualize the lid being removed, and jumping to freedom.

Rather than griping about your condition—do something.

Make a *Dig Your Work Action Plan.*

Part II
The Dig Your Work Action Plan

The Dig Your Work Action Plan

*One difference between successful people and all the
rest is that successful people take action.*
Bob Proctor

Rarely will you get results by waiting for things to
improve. You need a plan. Not much gets done in this
world without plans.

As you build your plan, emphasize the actions you
will take. Focus on one or two actions at once. Set
time goals for improvement, and interim checkpoints
to evaluate your progress.

**1. Make your list of improvements you want to
see.**
What do you not like at work? What would it look
like if you made improvements?

Say that you want more autonomy. Your boss holds
all the cards. You have not room to breathe. She
controls everything you do.

**What would it look like if you resolved this
issue?** She tells you *want* needs to be done,
not *how* to do it. She asks you to plan a new project,
rather than dictate. When issues arise, rather than take

full control, she allows you to resolve the issue and lets you simply keep her informed. You many want to set an ultimate resolution, and an acceptable one. You can shoot for the ideal, but you may have to settle for the acceptable one. Identify these two levels.

2. Determine type of resolution required.

Resolution types look like this:

a. Self-resolution actions.
You can take action and resolve these myself. For example, you want to reduce or eliminate your negative talking. These actions depend only on you, and you can take immediate action.

b. Speaking up actions.
You need to negotiate with your boss, coworker, or someone else to get their help, cooperation, or change. Achieving more freedom and autonomy from your boss will require speaking up.

c. Nibble actions.
You will take a few steps that should improve the negative situation. You have a strained relationship with a coworker and you resolve to work on improving this relationship. No one action will resolve this; you will need to take several small actions.

d. Learning actions.

You may not know precisely how to proceed, you need to improve some skills first. A good example of this type of action is learning to persuade your boss to loosen her micromanaging grip on you. But you feel you need to learn how to speak up assertively. You will probably need to find a book or seminar that will teach you assertiveness skills.

Some issues may require multiple resolution types. Brainstorm from six to twelve possible actions, evaluate their potential, and then select your top three.

3. Prioritize your improvements.
You may want to start with improvements that require self-resolution or nibble actions. On those improvements you can start immediately. The others will probably require more preparation.

4. Set time goals for acceptable resolution.
When would like to see this issue resolved? You may not see 100% resolution, but when would you like to see the issue resolved at the acceptable level.

5. Set checkpoints.
For each action, set time points at which you will evaluate improvement. Are you improving enough? Have you hit your acceptable improvement? If so, do you want to continue working toward your ideal resolution? If not, you may want to try implementing other actions you listed in step two.

The *Dig Your Work Action Plan* works. Remember, your first try may not bring the improvement you want, but don't give up. Keep working on approaches until you hit at least your acceptable resolution.

Quit Griping and Do Something

What we focus on and choose to see is what brings us feelings of joy or feelings of despair.

Lloyd Newell

As I mentioned at the beginning of this book, when I was unhappy with my employment, rather than do something about it, I complained. I'm not that unusual. Just listen to conversations between restaurant wait staff, store clerks, airline workers, or most any workers and you'll hear the complaints.

Unfortunately, when customers hear these discussions, they form a poor impression of your workplace and its staff.

Move your talk to action. What are you going to do about your dissatisfaction? If you focus helplessly on what you don't love about your work, you lose the will to improve.

The more you gripe, the less likely you'll act. So stop talking about it, and start your action list. What are you going to do?

Make your *Dig Your Work Action Plan.*

Part III

The Application of the Plan

Now we get to apply the *Dig Work Action Plan* to specific issues.

We address the issues in the order of importance per my research.

Your Boss

Control your own destiny or someone else will.

Jack Welch

According to my research, the number one issue that keeps employees from enjoying their work is ineffective or unsupportive leaders. My study participants report:

- Disorganization
- Poor communication
- Lack of autonomy
- Instability or changing priorities
- Lack of respect, trust, appreciation, and recognition
- Unethical or illegal behavior

Many people feel that they cannot speak up to their boss. And many of them are correct. Old-style bosses, those Stephen Covey calls *Industrial Age Managers*, communicate as senders not as receivers. They expect compliance. They control, press, micromanage, and chastise. Those who are unfortunate enough to work for these tyrants feel like they just show up and do what they're told. Their training, experience, creativity, and initiate sit idle while they comply.

If you find yourself in this horrible position, you aren't helpless; you have five choices:

- You can continue complying.
- You can speak up.
- You can challenge your boss.
- You can transfer to a better boss.
- You can leave your organization.

If you feel you want to speak up, I suggest you make an appointment. Be cautious about flaring up in the heat of a discussion. Have this conversation one-on-one, and at a time where your "speaking up" conversation is the only topic to be discussed.

Pre-live the Conversation

To be successful, you need to learn to really communicate with others.
John C. Maxwell

Before you visit with your boss, plan the conversation from beginning to end.

First, brainstorm several options for your opening statement. Write them down, eliminate the obvious losers, and make your top choice.

Second, think about every possible objection you could hear from your boss. List them.

Third, take each possible objection, and brainstorm your responses--shoot for a dozen answers per objection. Analyze each possible response, and select the most appropriate one.

Pre-living the conversation will give you better odds of getting the outcome you seek. Rather than

28

depending on coming up with good responses to objections in the moment, you prepare, ponder, and carefully choose your responses.

Also, you will feel more confidence and poise in the conversation because you feel prepared. Confidence helps you make your case. If you don't seem convinced, how can you convince your boss?

Find Reasons Your Boss Would Want to Help
Express the benefits to your organization or to your boss of accepting your proposal. Explain why he or she should work with you on your request.

Align your request with your boss's values: budget compliance, sales and revenue, quality product, customer service, or even family.

Identify Your Ideal and Acceptable Outcomes
Before you talk with your boss, determine your ideal outcome. What would be the best result you can expect?

Then, identify your lowest acceptable outcome.

Keep the conversation between these two outcomes.

Speaking of confidence, in any negotiation, expect to get what you're requesting. You truly get what you expect.

Magic Phrases

As you pre-live your conversation, plan to use these two magic phrases.

The first phrase will help you lead the conversation, "I need your help." This phrase sets the stage for cooperation. It shows humility and earnest concern. Your boss will more likely tune his or her ear to your request.

The second phrase will help you meet any objection, "I see it differently." I find this statement more effective than, "I disagree." You aren't making your boss wrong, you are just stating your point of view. You will generate less defensiveness, and engender more cooperation.

Equipped with these effective communication techniques, you will more likely reach your ideal outcome or an acceptable compromise.

Make Suggestions

Don't just complain; make real, viable suggestions. Anyone can complain. Show your boss that you've thought through several options. State the option you most favor.

On some issues, you can suggest a test of two or more options.

I once led a project of automating 360 nursing homes. None of these facilities, or their workers had ever used computers before. My team wrote, tested, implemented, and supported nineteen different business office and clinical applications. Our senior management team wanted our computer staff to train everyone, including the nurses. I objected, saying that nurses should teach nurses. Our IT team would have less credibility and would receive more resistance than an actual nurse.

The management wouldn't budge, so I proposed a test. One facility would receive the clinical training by our computer professionals. Nurses would teach another site. It didn't take long for the senior management to unanimously agree to my point.

Covey's Emotional Bank Account

I can live for two months on a good compliment.
                                        Mark Twain

Stephen Covey, in his historic book, *The 7 Habits of Highly Effective People*, describes a way that you can increase your influence on another. He calls his principle, "The Emotional Bank Account."

He compares the emotional bank account to your checking account. You make deposits and your checking account balance rises. You make withdrawals and the balance lowers. If you have a high balance and make a withdrawal, no problem. But if you have a low balance and make a withdrawal— consequences.

In your emotional bank account you have a balance with another individual. The higher the balance, the more influence you have. You also make deposits and withdrawals to this account, affecting the balance with the individual. You make deposits when you treat him or her with respect, tell the truth, do what you promise, get to know the person personally, and so forth. You make withdrawals when you do the opposites of these, and when you argue, communicate negatively, challenge decisions, or negotiate for what you want.

You will more likely get what you seek in negotiations or when you ask for help if you have a high balance. The relationship adds to the influence.

Make enough deposits and you're more likely to get what you need, and dig your work more.

Apply these principles to your relationship with your boss, and you can influence your way to digging your work.

Your Coworkers

Individuals who deliberately decide not to take offense lead happier, more productive lives.
                                        Lloyd Newell

My research shows that coworkers present the best and the second worst part of work. The work itself can be relatively predictable. People are not.

You may experience challenges like:
- Personality conflicts
- Negativity
- Blame
- Hurt feelings
- Competition
- Cultural differences
- Feuds between departments
- Stress
- An unfortunate history with a person

When faced with a tough person issue, we usually know things not to do; yet we often do them anyway. We want to save face, or simply act on our impulses rather than our rational mind. We worsen the situation.

What will it take to begin to improve your work relationships? Let's apply the *Dig Your Work Action Plan*.

1. I want to relax tensions between Peggy and me. What does that look like? Peggy no longer ambushes me in meetings. She tells the whole truth about our projects, rather than making herself look good, and making my team and me look like the slackers.

2. Resolution types:

> a. Self-resolution actions
> First look at yourself. Which of your actions contribute to the problem? This side of the tension is the simplest to improve. You can control yourself better than you can control others. You will probably find that fixing your actions and reactions toward others will ease the tension. People tend to relax when you relax.
>
> b. Speaking up actions
> You can meet with Peggy and discuss the issue and your history of conflicts. Solicit her

cooperation. Be sure to pre-live this conversation. Ask to sit down once a month to discuss your improvements.

c. Nibble actions
You can pay sincere compliments on improvements you see Peggy making. You can go to lunch together. Chocolate usually works as a good peacemaker.

d. Learning actions
You may choose to pick up a book on personal conflict resolution, or Dale Carnegie's *How to Win Friends and Influence People*.

Don't forget to pre-live your conversations.

Now let's discuss some other actions to improve your coworker relationships.

Ain't It Awful Club

Complainers are crap magnets.
T. Harv Eker

Jack Canfield tells about his discovery of the *Ain't It Awful Club*. As a new high school history teacher, he found the club having its meetings in the teachers' lounge. On the agenda:

- Students
- Parents
- Administration
- Pay
- Budget and supplies
- Textbooks
- Curriculum
- Testing requirements
- Facilities
- Janitors
- Lunch ladies

He points out that every organization has an *Ain't It Awful Club*. In my long career I have worked only one place that had no *Ain't It Awful Club*—I'm self-employed.

Canfield and I challenge you to stay out of the club. Steer to more positive or at least neutral conversations.

The more you focus on the negative, the less you will dig your work.

You don't have to scold the complainers, just change the subject.

A few years ago I led breakout sessions at a church single adult conference. At noon I sat at a round table to enjoy a sandwich. In a few minutes all the other seats were filled with nine women.

Immediately these single women started talking about their ex-husbands. Do you think that conversation was positive? Like a bunch of guys telling fishing stories, these women competed for the most sensational ex-husband sin.

First I looked around to see if any of the nearby tables had any vacancies. Then I decided to see if I could turn the conversation. At the next pause I spoke up, "What have you learned at your conference so far?"

The energy at the table immediately revved up. They became animated and excited to tell what they experienced.

That positive energy continued for the rest of the hour without requiring a second boost. As they dispersed to return to their next sessions, I heard one tell the other, "Wasn't that fun?" Do you think she would have said that if they'd continued comparing their deadbeat ex-husbands?

Avoid toxic people and their clubs.

Avoid TV News

Nourish the mind like you would your body. The mind
cannot survive on junk food.

Jim Rohn

For years I've read of thought leaders who recommended we turn off the television news. That always concerned me. I want to stay informed about the issues of the day.

But the more I have observed I see that the principle of avoiding the television news has merit.

Every news outlet has a point of view. They try to mask it, but it's there.

They need to report on the most salacious stories in order to attract viewers. Then they sensationalize the stories to keep you coming back.

Television news is presented serially, meaning you have to watch stories of the lowest order (murders, crimes, scandals, and corruption) before you get to hear about your interests.

When you get your news from the Internet you can get multiple points of view. You can also jump right to the stories that interest you and skip the latest celebrity scandal.

Think of your media experience as a meal. Do you want to take in junk food laden with empty calories and fat, or would you rather take in a balanced meal that contributes to your health and leaves you feeling energized?

You pick.

Offer Sincere praise

I can live for two months on a good compliment.
Mark Twain

People respond to sincerely given praise. Most people like to hear recognition for what they do well. Sincere praise can bridge divisions between people.

A negative person may feel suspicious of you at first. Make sure you really feel the compliment you give. It can't be effective if it's not a true expression. Insincere praise is manipulation.

You get what you expect
Have you noticed how some people seem to have all the luck? They persuade people to do what they want. They get all the breaks.

They even win stuff. Some people win door prizes and other drawings beyond the laws of probability. I'm one of those.

I've won computers, luggage, gift bags, cash, and a car. At an association conference in San Diego, attended by 12,000 members, I won the big prize--a $500 American Express gift card. The next year I attended their meeting in Orlando. Even more members attended. I won it again. Two years in a row, 24,000 people, and I won the largest prize both times.

As a kid I won a few prizes—a garbage disposal and two helicopter trips with Santa.

Because I won as a kid, I started to expect to win.

So what does winning door prizes have to do with digging your work?

If you worry about what might happen, or if you focus on those bad things, you increase the likelihood of them happening. I don't understand the physics of this principle, but I've seen it in action many times.

Expect your boss to make decisions in your favor. Expect cooperation from your coworkers. Expect negotiations to go your way.

You truly get what you expect.

Stress and Time Constraints

Time management is really life management. It's a skill that can be learned.

Brian Tracy

We have received warnings for decades about the long-term effects of stress. Yet the velocity of its increase continues. We know that people do higher quality work, and even have higher productivity when their stress levels are kept at manageable levels.

Higher stress over long periods produces illness, and even death. Heart disease, obesity, insomnia, depression, and many other illnesses count stress among its causes. The effects in the workplace include: absenteeism, employee turnover, conflict, burnout, angry outbursts, bullying, poor attitudes, change resistance, and emotional exhaustion. Family issues often result, multiplying the stress.

How can you dig your work when faced with such high levels of stress?

First you can identify the main sources of your stress?
Some common sources include:

- Unreasonable deadlines or expectations
- Conflict
- Time constraints
- Lack of autonomy
- Mishandled changes
- Problem customers, clients, and patients
- Excessive overtime

Learn Away Your Stress

Many times the reading of a book has made the future of a man.
Ralph Waldo Emerson

I've observed that most work stress comes from two sources:

- You feel trapped as if you have no options
- You find yourself in a situation you don't know how to handle

You're rarely really trapped. You have options. You can:
- Speak up
- Negotiate
- Learn how to handle the situation
- Look for other positions or employers

When you don't know how to handle a situation, you can learn how to handle it. Learn away your stress. Hate conflict? Learn how to handle it. Need to speak up for yourself more? Learn negotiation and assertive communication. Don't have enough time to do all of your work? Learn time management techniques. You get the idea.

Look at your list of things you dislike about your job, and learn what you need to learn to improve them.

Sound easy? It will take time, but the payoff is worth it.

Tell the Truth

Your character will always eclipse your talent.
Tamara Lowe

Tell the truth and tell it early.

Too many employees hide issues, hoping they can figure them out before they are exposed. Big mistake. Hiding issues complicates their resolution. It adds to your stress. It hurts your credibility.

When an issue arises, one of your first thoughts should be, "Who needs to know about this?"

Be careful to be truthful, avoid exaggerating or minimizing impacts.

If you have a solid reputation for truth telling, your influence rises.

When you make a mistake, turn yourself in immediately.

Telling the truth lowers stress.

Keep a Master To-do List

Do not let what you can't do interfere with what you can do.

John Wooden

Do you find it tough to keep track of every task you need to do? You're not alone. Important tasks get left undone. You feel stress as you try to remember everything on your plate.

Keep a master to-do list and you will solve the missed task issue and lower your stress.

Start a list of every task you need to do. Don't worry about prioritizing the tasks; just get them down.

Keep this list in one place. Avoid posting sticky notes everywhere. Years ago I kept my master to-do list in my paper planner. Then I moved it to a pocket binder. Now I use the Evernote® app on my smart phone.

It may seem like a simple and easy tip, but by keeping your master to-do list you save yourself much grief and embarrassment.

Focused Hours

What we focus on expands. If we focus on the problems in our lives, they tend to increase. If we focus on the good things we already have, they too, have a tendency to grow.

Michael Angier

Are you frustrated that you can't get your work finished because of interruptions? Just as you get in a good working zone, a coworker pops in, the phone rings, or your e-mail notifies you of one more message.

I've read multiple studies that quantify the effect on your productivity. One study claims that it takes you eight minutes after the interruption is over to get back into a good working zone. Another study says the time to recover is twenty-five minutes. If you add up your daily interruptions, you should find somewhere between thirty and forty. And many more if you treat e-mail like instant messaging.

You need to take some control over your time.

Try using focused hours. Select a few tasks you need to accomplish, especially tasks that will require deep focus. Then plot out on your calendar hour-long blocks when you will work on each one. Monday from 2-3 p.m. I'll work on this task. On Tuesday from 10-11 a.m. I'll work on this one. Mark yourself "busy" during these hours. Consider these focused hours as if you were holding meetings with yourself.

You may think, "I can't do that where I work." You need to do this most of all. Your workday is probably one stimulus and response after another. Take some control. No wonder you're stressed out.

Come up with an appropriate signal to alert those around you, "I should not be disturbed unless you have an emergency." The signal could be a closed door. You could make a sign. Make sure the sign is polite; you're trying to get cooperation. If you work in a cubicle, yellow police caution tape across the cubicle entrance will work.

Of course, you need to train people on what constitutes an emergency.

During your focused hour, let your phone calls go to voicemail as if you were in a meeting. Shutdown e-mail.

It's amazing how much work you can accomplish in a focused, uninterrupted hour!

The benefits of using focused hours are many:

- You get much more work done
- Your work quality improves
- You lower your stress because you know exactly when you'll work on your important tasks
- You become nicer to your coworkers and staff, because their interruptions come at better times

Try it; you'll like it.

Does Your E-mail Control You?

We cannot waste time without bruising eternity.
Lloyd Newell

Who's the boss here? Who controls whom? Does your e-mail inbox control your time or do you? Do you treat e-mail like instant messaging? When you receive that inbox notification, do you interrupt your work and read it?

If your e-mail inbox serves as your master, I suggest you lead a coup d'état.

Studies suggest that it takes us from eight to 25 minutes after an interruption is completed to get back into a good working zone. They also say that 40% of the time, we can't remember what we had been doing before the interruption and thus we move on to something else.

Take control of your e-mail. Schedule when you'll check it, and shut it down at other times. You may need to inform those around you so they know to come to your office if they need an immediate response.

It's amazing what you can accomplish when you focus on your current task and not receive that digital nudge every few minutes.

Find a Passionate Purpose

Think big and dream big if you want to be big.
Albert Mensah

The money we make brings little lasting satisfaction. We love receiving raises, but once we become accustomed to the new pay rate, we lose enthusiasm for it.

Every one of us needs a passionate purpose.

So what brings you a sense of purpose? Do you feel passion about your customers, clients, or patients? Do you feel passion for building up those whom you lead? Do you feel it for the deep purpose served by your organization?

Try to avoid dwelling only on the mundane annoyances and troubles of your work. Lift your vision to your passionate purpose.

Write a one-sentence passionate purpose statement.

"I leave my wife and home 180 days per year, sleeping in low-cost, and low-class hotels, eating their free breakfast carbs, presenting material that 95% of my audience members won't even apply."

Would that make you want to head to the airport for another week of speaking? Would that make you get up in the morning raring to present your material? Me either. Read my real passionate purpose statement.

"I teach more than 180 audiences per year how to take accountability for their job happiness, and hundreds of people actually do it."

Applying the *Dig Your Work Plan* to Lower Your Stress

Accomplishment follows activity.

David DeFord

Let's use the Dig Work Action Plan to lower your stress.

1. List your sources of stress
     a. Time constraints

     b. Unreasonable expectations

     c. Micromanaging boss

     d. Overtime requirements

2. Prioritize
     a. Let's tackle the time constraints because they have relationships with the other sources.

What does success look like?

Ideal: You enjoyed a refreshing ten-minute break mid-morning and mid-afternoon, you took a full lunch period, and you left work at an acceptable time. **Acceptable:** You leave work at the end of the day with fewer tasks than you had at the beginning of the day.

3. Action Types

    a. **Self-resolution actions**

        1. Begin applying the Focused Hours approach as described earlier.

        2. Limit the number and duration of drop-in visits.

    b. **Speaking up actions**

        1. Talk with your boss about your workload. Come prepared with suggestions.

    c. **Nibble actions**

        1. Create a Master To-do List to reduce forgotten tasks

        2. Cut down on alcohol uses you have a clearer mind

        3. Consciously make deposits into the emotional bank account with your boss

    d. **Learning actions**

1. Read *Getting Things Done* by David Allen
2. Read a book about saying "no"

4. Time Goals

At the end of thirty days you expect a noticeable improvement in restedness, an increase of four hours more family time per week, and five fewer master to-do list items

5. Interim Checkpoint

Every Friday evaluate your progress. Adjust the plan as needed.

Especially for Leaders

A leader who treats people right will find that the right kind of people are drawn to his or her organization.

John Wooden

I hate to tell you, but you are the number one reason your staff doesn't like their work. Oh well, you aren't there to make friends. But the impact of poor leadership seriously affects your team.

Ineffective and unsupportive leaders increase turnover, lower productivity, throttle initiative, heighten conflict, and generate greater negativity.

The only unity weak leaders generate is the common hatred toward them. In fact, if a team member defends you, they find themselves on the outs with their teammates. This "us vs. them" mentality produces nothing positive.

Covey describes differences between what he calls, "industrial age managers" and "information age leaders." Old-school, industrial age managers lead harshly, make all of the decisions, lead one-way communication meetings, bark orders, and isolate themselves from their "subordinates." These managers try to increase productivity by driving their underlings.

Information age leaders show genuine interest in their people. They persuade rather than order. They collaborate with their teams, respecting the suggestions of their "associates." These leaders increase productivity by trusting their teams, and giving them autonomy.''

These leaders actually produce more work through their teams than the old-school managers.

What do old-style managers do to drain the energy out of their teams?

- They kill productivity and morale through their meetings
- They falsely elevate the urgency of work
- They show their distrust of their teams by micromanaging them
- They only show interest in team members' growth during the annual reviews

- They communicate primarily what their people do wrong

Let's explore actions you can take to minimize these energy drainers.

Your Meetings Can Add to Rather Than Drain Productivity

The single biggest factor between being okay and being magnificent is taking full responsibility for what you are experiencing.

Kody Bateman

Your meetings hurt productivity and morale when you:

- Hold too many meetings
- Don't start or end on time
- Include the wrong people
- Vary from the agenda
- Don't publish an agenda
- Allow long-talkers, high-jackers, dominators, and loopers
- Have the meeting just because you always have the meeting
- Allow one or two people to dominate the discussion
- Allow ambushing and attacking

- Use meetings to waste your team members' time while saving your time
- Copy/paste the agenda causing you to have the same meeting week after week

Some people lead solely through meetings. They save their own time, while killing their team members' time. I consider this a selfish practice.

If you have ten team members, and each discusses his topic for ten minutes. You have killed more than an hour and a half of important time that could have been used to do real work. Multiply that hour and a half times the ten attendees and you realize you just killed fifteen people hours. If this meeting is held each week, you lose 780 hours of production. That's expensive.

Convert this meeting to one-on-one discussions and you save hundreds of hours per year. Of course, you'll want to meet occasionally, but many of your regular meetings could be replaced.

Remember, the value of the meeting should exceed the cost.

Here are some guidelines you may want to consider to freshen and give energy to your meetings.

Start and End on Time

Respect the people who arrive on time by starting when you say you will start. Don't wait for others to show.

If you wait you train people to arrive late.

Never recap previously discussed information for your tardy attendees. Let them find out what was covered before they arrived from a friend, or let them read the record.

Most people consider that when you allow your meetings to run later than published you show them disrespect. I agree. People have too much to do to rob them of more time than they committed.

Plus, many people have meetings immediately after your meeting. When you run late, you're making them choose between leaving your meeting before it closes and arriving late to their next meeting.

Meeting Prep

Let's say that you hold a regular meeting every Thursday at 2 p.m. Your team consists of ten people.

The most important day related to your Thursday meeting is Tuesday. On this day you will make some decisions and take some actions.

First, decide if you want to have the meeting at all this time. If your people are in the throes of a project, and their productive time needs to be protected, maybe the cost of the meeting isn't worth the value.

Occasionally canceling a meeting shows respect for your team members' time. Be careful to not cancel too often. They may stop protecting that time on their calendars.

The second decision you can make on Tuesday is who needs to attend this time. Look at your agenda topics and decide which of your team members need to attend. You can excuse those who have no concern for the topics to be covered, or those who have heavy commitments this week.

Some people don't like it when you exclude them. They think of your meetings like recess. They get to rest from their work, and they can daydream about other things. Also, they may feel worried that you're talking about them. Make sure you send the agenda and meeting record to them.

The third decision for Tuesday is who should be there the whole time. If a person currently has tight time commitments, you can have her attend for the agenda topics that affect her, and excuse her before you cover the topics that don't.

The main actions you may perform on Tuesday, two days before the meeting, are prepare and distribute the agenda.

The Agenda

Consider including at least these three pieces of information on your agenda:

1. Detailed description of each topic
2. Names of the people to discuss each topic
3. The time allotted for the topics

If you copy/paste your agenda from week to week, you essentially hold the same meeting, with the same discussion, with the same conclusions each week. Be very detailed on your agenda topic descriptions. This will help your discussion begin where you would like. Also, your people will know what to prepare and what to bring.

List the names of each person who should discuss each topic. If you have a detailed description and the names you will have fewer people come to your meetings unprepared.

Have you noticed that the unprepared people talk the longest? They keep talking, hoping that something brilliant will come out. But they are pumping dry wells.

Timed Agendas

Most meetings would improve if you use a timed agenda. Try to keep your meetings to no longer than one hour. After an hour, attention decreases and people lose concentration. Consider timing your meeting for 45 minutes on the initial agenda sent out two days prior to the meeting. This will allow you to make adjustments as members ask for more time on their topics, and will make it convenient if you decide to add a topic.

If you use clock time rather than duration, the attendees will help you stay on track.

Meeting Roles

You may choose to have three roles in your meeting:
1. Meeting leader
2. Timekeeper
3. Record keeper

You may serve as the meeting leader, or you may appoint someone who would naturally attend the meeting. Think of your team members who would like to grow into a leadership position. Successful leaders need to know how to lead meetings. You can help your people grow by giving them opportunities to lead your meetings.

Too many meeting leaders try to serve as timekeeper and record keeper also. Ask others to fill these two roles. The leader's responsibility is to keep the meeting flowing. If you're trying to serve in these other roles, you'll get distracted.

Be sure to ask the recorder and the timekeeper in advance. They'll need to come prepared, and they will need to stay after the meeting for another ten minutes.

The Recorder
The only attendee allowed to bring a toy is the recorder. This person will type the record as the meeting progresses.

See that the recorder captures at least these important items:

1. Reported Status

If members report their status on a project, see that this information gets added to the record.

2. Decisions
Record these. If it's not written, it wasn't decided.

3. Action Items
I consider action items the most important outcomes of meetings. See that these not only get recorded, but also placed in a section at the top of the record. Try to avoid mixing action items among the other information.

People typically read one-third of what you write—usually the top third. By putting the action items at the top, they are less likely to be missed.

How to Get People to Participate
Why do people not participate?

1. They may feel disinterested.
Either disinvite them, or have them only attend the portion of the meeting that pertains to them.

2. They may feel shy.

This usually means the person lacks self-esteem in that setting. Make it safe for their participation by insisting that respectful discussion is required.

3. They may fear that if they speak up, they'll receive a new assignment.
    Try to avoid the pattern of always tagging the suggestion-giver with the responsibility to carry out the suggestion.

4. They may be "processors."
    These people think deeply. They may still be processing the information from two or three agenda topics back. By the time they have something to say, you're discussing new topics.
    If you have team members who process, you may want to invite them two days ahead, when you send out the agenda, to think about the topic. You may give them additional information and ask them to be prepared to discuss. This allows them to process the information before the meeting begins.

5. They may have been shot down in the past when they spoke up.
    Again, insist on respectful discussions.

Long-talkers, Loopers, and High-jackers

These people dominate your meetings. They take forever to explain themselves. They re-explain the same point several times. Or they take the conversation in a direction you didn't intend. They digress.

What's a meeting leader to do?

You have several options.

1. You can embarrass them in the meeting. They will feel that they have to save face, so they may act out. This can turn ugly quickly.

2. You may give permission to everyone in the room to point out that the discussion has digressed.
   You may want to do this in a light, nonthreatening way. For instance, I heard of teams creating a keyword that anyone in the room may call out when the discussion has digressed. They use words like, "Cabbage," "Muskrat," or "Rabbits."
   I've heard of others who place a 5" X 8" card facedown at everyone's place. The card has the word, "ELMO" printed on it. When a

diversion occurs, anyone may hold up his or her card. "ELMO" stands for "Enough, Let's Move On."

3. You may choose to talk privately with the consistent digresser and ask for his or her help in keeping the meeting on track.
4. Lastly, you may choose to appoint the windbag as timekeeper. I think you see why.

Toys

Shoot for "Toy-free" meetings. Tell people to stow their phones, tablets, and laptops so they can fully focus and participate.

Toy-use creates costly distractions; causes people to miss information, and may cause you to waste valuable time repeating what's already been covered. Only the recorder may bring a laptop.

After the Meeting

Try having the timekeeper and recorder stay with you for ten additional minutes. You can perform two important tasks.

1. The three of you can review the typed record and make any changes you agreed on. Then have the recorder e-mail the record immediately. That way the right people

receive the written record within five minutes of the meeting's end.

2. Discuss what went well, and what could be improved. This brief meeting evaluation will help you make adjustments so you can continually improve.

Five-year Goals

*Make no small plans. They have no magic to stir
men's souls.*
Spencer W. Kimball

Learn what your team members want five years from
now. Do they want job growth? Do they want to learn
new skills? Ask them.

Once you know what they want to do or learn, clear
the path for them.

Consider what they need to experience or study to
achieve their desires. Look for opportunities to give
them appropriate assignments to prepare them for
what they want. When considering delegating a task
to someone, think, "Who needs this experience?"

Suggest books or training your team members can
acquire to help them prepare for what they want.

If your funding falls short of providing these
materials and training for them, challenge them to

own their careers and pursue the training and books themselves.

Follow up regularly to review your team members' progress. Show genuine interest. Give valuable guidance in their pursuit of these goals.

Mastermind Groups

You are the same today as you will be five years from now except for two things: the people you meet and the books you read.
Charles "Tremendous" Jones

Leadership can feel pretty lonely sometimes. You need to stay fresh, collaborate with other leaders, and freely discuss your challenges with others who might understand.

Forming a mastermind group can provide the inspiration and guidance you need to move forward. Ask two or three other leaders to meet regularly to collaborate for each other's success.

Invite participants who are leaders from other industries who you know from church, your service organization, or from your previous places of employment.

You can meet by phone or in person. Weekly, bi-weekly, or monthly meetings may work best.

A typical mastermind group meeting agenda includes two simple topics:

1. Wins for the week
   What went well? Allow yourself to brag a little here. As each of you discusses your successes, you set the tone for future performance. It also provides extra incentive to create some wins about which you can brag.

   Celebrate each other's successes.

2. Discuss a challenge
   Collaborate together on your challenges. With group members who don't feel close to the situation, you will receive creative, "stretching the box" suggestions.
   Solutions to your challenges may appear obvious to those not mired them.

I have enjoyed my participation in several mastermind groups over the years. My colleagues inspired me, challenged me, advised me, and occasionally chastised me when I needed it.

Study Leadership the Rest of Your Life

A leader who is through learning is through. And so is the team he leads.

John Wooden

Study leadership the rest of your life.

You will learn from those who lead you throughout your career. But if you limit your understanding of leadership to the examples you observe from your leaders, you greatly limit your scope of leadership understanding.

Learn from the world's best leaders.

Some excellent books, audios, and videos await your attention.

I have included many of my favorite leadership books in Part IV. Purchase those that you feel will guide you to greater skill and work satisfaction.

Part IV

Learn What You Need to Learn

Commit yourself to lifelong learning. The most valuable asset you'll ever have is your mind and what you put into it.

Brian Tracy

Most people who love their work especially love to improve. They find new ways to do their duties. They ask others for ideas, they take classes, and they read.

I highly recommend the following books. You will find links to Amazon on these books and an updated list at http://www.DavidDeFord.com/dywbooks

Make Your Life a Masterpiece, David DeFord
I Wish to Be Useful, David DeFord
The Success Principles, Jack Canfield
The Achievement Code, Michael Angier
The Think Big Manifesto, Michael Post
Getting Things Done, David Allen
The No Complaining Rule, Jon Gordon

No Excuses, Brian Tracy

The Power of Nice, Linda Kaplan Thaler and Robin Koval

Persuasion: The Art of Getting What You Want, Dave Lakhani

The Likeability Factor, Tim Sanders

Think and Grow Rich, Napoleon Hill

The Servant: A Simple Story About the True Essence of Leadership, James Hunter

Manage Your Day-to-Day: Build Your Routine, Find Your Focus, and Sharpen Your Creative Mind, Jocelyn Glei

The ONE Thing, Gary Keller and Jay Papasan

Everything I Know About Business I Learned from the Grateful Dead: The Ten Most Innovative Lessons from a Long, Strange Trip, Barry Barnes

Ctrl Alt Delete: Reboot Your Business. Reboot Your Life. Your Future Depends on It. Mitch Joel

The 15 Invaluable Laws of Growth: Live Them and Reach Your Potential, John C. Maxwell

The Power of Self-Confidence: Become Unstoppable, Irresistible, and Unafraid in Every Area of Your Life, Brian Tracy

How Will You Measure Your Life?, Clayton Christensen

Conclusion

People become really quite remarkable when they start thinking that they can do things. When they believe in themselves they have the first secret of success.

Norman Vincent Peale

At the end of each year, I hope you deeply reflect on your work and the impact you have on others.

I wish for you rewarding and meaningfully rich experiences in your career. These beautiful experiences come from taking control, taking action, and taking responsibility for your own work happiness.

I hope you Dig Your Work.

www.ingramcontent.com/pod-product-compliance
Lightning Source LLC
Chambersburg PA
CBHW071611170526
45166CB00003B/1056